HISTO
YARMOUTH
TOWN *&* COUNTY

Eric Ruff *and* Laura Bradley

NIMBUS
PUBLISHING LTD

AND THE YARMOUTH COUNTY MUSEUM

Nimbus Publishing Limited
PO Box 9301, Station A
Halifax, NS B3K 5N5
(902) 455-4286
Co-published with the Yarmouth County Museum
22 Collins Street
Yarmouth, NS B5A 3C8
(902) 742-5539

Design: Joan Sinclair
Printed and bound in Canada

Canadian Cataloguing in Publication Data
Ruff, Eric
Historic Yarmouth
ISBN 1-55109-220-4
1. Yarmouth (N.S.)—History—Pictorial works.
2. Yarmouth (N.S.: County)—History—Pictorial works.
I. Bradley, Laura.   II. Title.
FC2349.Y3R85 1997   971.6'31'00222   C97-950170-9
F1039.5.Y3R85 1997

Front cover: The little girl in the tree is Kathryn Ladd, daughter of Captain Fred Ladd. Although she was raised primarily at sea, she came home to Yarmouth regularly, and developed lifelong friendships here.

Back cover: Parker-Eakin's wharf in Yarmouth. (See pages 36–37.)

Title page: Streetcar on Main Street at the corner of John Street, Yarmouth. From August 6, 1892, when Yarmouth operated the first streetcar railway east of Montreal, until the 1920s, citizens could travel in comfort from the Argyle Street corner in the South End to Milton Corner, or, in the summer, to Murphy's Bridge (now the Villa St. Joseph).

Acknowledgments

We would like to thank a number of people for their assistance.
First, we are grateful to the managing editor at Nimbus, Dorothy Blythe, for her invitation to discuss the idea of this book and for her continued support throughout the project. Joan Sinclair, also from Nimbus, designed and oversaw production of this book, and earned our sincere appreciation.

We also offer our thanks to several people who assisted with specific subject areas: Linda Campbell who helped with the architectural chapters; Bruce Ellis of the Army Museum; Vaughn Bullerwell who researched the Businesses and Public Architecture chapters; Fred Watkins who offered advice on technical terms relating to oxen; and Dr. Susan Young for information on Gordon Hatfield.

Thanks to various members of the Museum and Archives staff and volunteers, including Nathan Bain, Jena Pitman and Janice Stelma for their research assistance; and Helen Hall whose research notes and articles on Yarmouth photographers were invaluable.

Finally, we extend our deep gratitude to all those who have donated photographs to our marvellous collection.

Laura Bradley and Eric Ruff

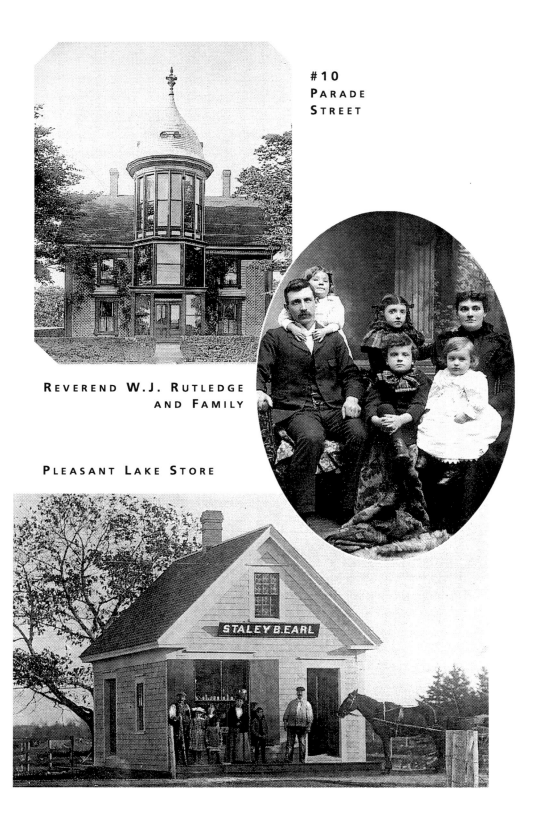

#10 PARADE STREET

REVEREND W.J. RUTLEDGE AND FAMILY

PLEASANT LAKE STORE

STALEY B. EARL

Contents

INTRODUCTION   VI

CHAPTER 1
    STREETSCAPES   1

CHAPTER 2
    DOMESTIC ARCHITECTURE   13

CHAPTER 3
    BUSINESSES   25

CHAPTER 4
    PUBLIC ARCHITECTURE   41

CHAPTER 5
    SPECIAL EVENTS, SPORTS &   53
    LEISURE

CHAPTER 6
    UNIFORMS   65

CHAPTER 7
    SHIPPING   75

CHAPTER 8
    TRANSPORTATION   95

CHAPTER 9
    PHOTOGRAPHERS AND THEIR   103
    SUBJECTS

#10 Parade Street. In 1862 John W. Lovitt announced to his seafaring son, Captain John Lovitt, that this home was being built for the Captain's occupancy upon his return to Yarmouth. Captain John Lovitt, master mariner, was also involved in the family's shipping business and politics. The prominent glass tower, intended to serve as a greenhouse, was not added until 1891. The addition of the tower with nautical portholes in the dome made the home unique in the province and it has been a local landmark and tourist attraction ever since. The home remained in the Lovitt family from 1862 to 1995.

Reverend W .J. Rutledge and family. Rutledge was the minister at the Baptist Church at Port Maitland from 1901 to 1905. *Parker photograph*

Pleasant Lake Store. Staley B. Earle was born in Pleasant Lake in 1864. He ran this tiny grocery store. He died, apparently umarried, in 1916 at the age of 52.

Introduction

Although the Vikings may have visited the shores near Yarmouth about 1000 AD, the first certain evidence of a European presence in the area was Champlain's arrival in 1604, when he named Cape Forchu and explored the harbour. Certainly some settlement was made in the surrounding countryside by the Mi'kmaq and Acadians, but generally 1761 is regarded as the founding date of the Town of Yarmouth.

From 1761 the Yarmouth area was settled by New Englanders from Massachusetts, enticed to come by the offer of free land grants from a government aiming to populate the Nova Scotia mainland with settlers loyal to the Crown. The land grants were meant to resettle the lands left vacant by the expelled Acadians, although New Englanders came to other areas in the province, including present-day Yarmouth and county.

With the exception of one family that set up a mill at Cape Forchu Falls (now Milton), the early settlers made their homesteads at Chebogue. As the population grew with the migration of more New Englanders— many were relatives and friends of those first settlers—settlement moved steadily northward, through Kelley's Cove and Sand Beach to Church Hill and Yarmouth.

While the New England settlers in the Annapolis Valley turned to the soil for their livelihood, the rocky landscape of the Yarmouth area forced local folk to search elsewhere. The sea filled the need—and more. It provided fish as well as a means to transport it to markets abroad. The forest at the settlers' backs provided goods in the form of lumber for export and materials for shipbuilding.

Hailing from Massachusetts, it was only natural that the early inhabitants should trade with Boston for the manufactured goods they required. Gradually this trade expanded to include the West Indies, Saint John, and Halifax. Typical cargoes were wood or salt fish to the West Indies, sugar, rum, molasses, or salt from the West Indies to Boston or Saint John, then home to Yarmouth with manufactured goods.

As the skills and markets for shipbuilding, navigation, and commerce improved and broadened, so did the size of Yarmouth's fleet. And as the fleet grew, so did the number of ports visited by Yarmouth ships and their masters; the burgeoning town became well known throughout the shipping world. Indeed, in 1879, when Yarmouth reached its peak as a ship-owning port, the town was the second largest port of registry in Canada in terms of tonnage. (Saint John was the leader.) At this time, Canada was the fourth leading maritime nation in the world behind

Great Britain, the United States, and Norway.

The 1870s and 1880s were decades of great prosperity and growth for Yarmouth. Attractive public buildings such as churches and schools were built while industries and businesses flourished. Cultural life and recreation were also nurtured—there were literary societies, musical and theatrical groups, and sports organizations. Evidence of the wealth accumulated by Yarmouth's ship-owning merchants and seafarers still exists today in the large, elaborate houses and buildings, both in residential areas of town and along the main streets.

The shipping industry, which was largely responsible for such prosperity, gave rise, directly and indirectly, to a number of businesses and industries, some of which are still in operation. Included were shipyards, boat shops, block-making shops and all the other segment industries of shipbuilding, chandlers and suppliers, repair facilities, ship smiths, and foundries. The latter, initially established to provide cast-iron fittings for ships, branched out into the production of diverse items including stoves and kitchen ranges. One foundry, the Burrell-Johnson Iron Co., even produced complicated marine engines, sometimes the complete vessel, and later, shells for wartime use.

YARMOUTH HOTEL

This brick building with a three-storey bay window was built c. 1865 as the Yarmouth Hotel. The building was owned by Mrs. R. Balfour Brown, wife of a well-known Yarmouth cartoonist. In later years the building was called the American Hotel and currently houses businesses at the street level and apartments on the upper levels. This building is located on Main Street, at the end of Cliff Street.

Yarmouth businessmen wisely reinvested their money as sailing vessels gradually gave way to steamers in the nineteenth century. A major industry was established in the Yarmouth Duck and Yarn Company. Dominion Textiles, the descendant of that company, was a mainstay of Yarmouth's industry until 1991. Although greatly overshadowed by the glory of the square-riggers, Yarmouth's fishing vessels and the fishing industry itself were, and still are, important to the local economy.

Another of today's major industries, tourism, began with the creation of several steamship lines which operated vessels between Yarmouth and Boston. Freight such as blueberries and fish was carried along with passengers. With the development of the Dominion Atlantic Railway a fast service between Halifax and Boston or New York was established, and Yarmouth served as the change-over location to become known as the "Gateway to Nova Scotia." To manage the influx of travellers, the Grand Hotel was established, along with the vacation hotels of Markland and Bayview situated across the harbour.

Historic Yarmouth nicely complements this historical overview of the town and county of the same name. Perhaps because they reveal minute details of our past, these photographs—taken between the mid-1800s and the early 1940s, and almost all by professional photographers from Yarmouth—create a vivid impression of the town and county. Included here are main street scenes from Yarmouth and from several of the county's villages; scenes from special events that took place in the county; photographs of ships that made a name for Yarmouth at the height of the age of sail; the transition in modes of transportation; the houses and buildings in which local folk lived and worked; and photographs of the townspeople themselves.

In Paris during January 1839, L. J. M. Daguerre first announced that he had discovered a photographic process. By 1841 a photographer was advertising his business as close as Saint John, New Brunswick. Photography arrived in Yarmouth later that decade. Our collection at the Yarmouth County Museum Archives contains some of these early daguerrotypes. The Archives' photographic collection, which numbers approximately twenty thousand images and negatives, provides a wealth of detail about the history of Yarmouth, town and county, and its former inhabitants.

Over the years the museum has held a number of exhibits relating to photography—some have come as travelling exhibits, but the ones which appealed most to our visitors have been those with images relating to Yarmouth. These have included The Past in Focus, The Bob Brooks Exhibit, and The Doritt Horton Exhibit. As well, photographs from our collection have been shown in exhibits across Canada, in the United States, and in Europe, and they have appeared in numerous books and magazines.

For many years, the museum and archival staff have dreamed about a book of photographs from our collection, and we were delighted with this opportunity. Selecting two hundred or so photographs from our vast archival collection has been a most interesting and challenging task.

Subject areas and dates restricted our choices significantly and the quality and condition of many images reduced this number even further. However, choosing one photo over another was still agonizing. How often did we say, "We'll have to use that one in the *next* book"?

One thought kept recurring during this selection process: the quality of the photographs is superb. Today's photographs, aside from those we see in advertisements, travel magazines, and so on, are not taken by professional photographers. We are much more accustomed to snapshots taken by family and friends.

The photographers, whose images appear in this book, were documenting history while they were photographing houses, businesses, and families, as well as streetscapes of our town and surrounding villages, and other subjects. Their business was photography, and since they made money from their product they had to be good.

One chapter of this book features photographs of unidentified people, taken by several of Yarmouth's studio photographers. (If any reader should spot an ancestor we would be delighted to know about it.) We have included this chapter to bring attention to the number of photographers who have contributed significantly to our understanding of our past; however, not all of Yarmouth's early professional photographers are represented. Some excelled at outdoor shots of building exteriors rather than the "studio portraits" we were focusing on—or perhaps our collection does not include their best studio shots.

While this collection of images is just a small sampling of what our Archives contain, it is a good representative sample of our photographs, and perhaps of life itself in our past. Many pictures will be recognizable since the buildings are still there, others will bring back fond memories and, we hope, lead to reminiscing about life "in the good old days." The detail in the following photographs is amazing. We hope that looking at each image will be a rewarding experience and that people will enjoy this book of memories.

Eric Ruff
Yarmouth, Nova Scotia, 1997

Chapter 1

Streetscapes

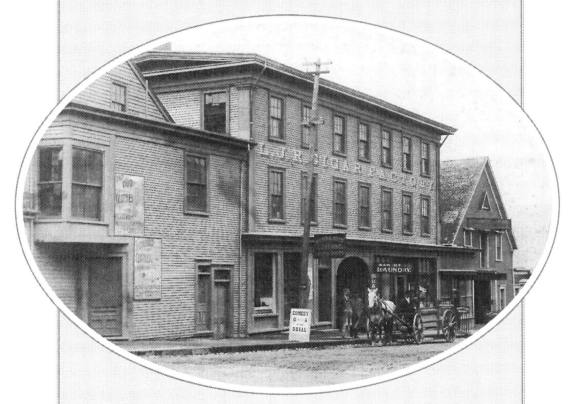

BROWN STREET

In the early 1900s the south side of Brown Street thrived. The L. J. Roy Cigar Factory, Sam Kee Laundry, a restaurant and livery stable all drew customers to Brown Street. The billboard advertising "Comedy Gymnasts at the Royal" is an unexpected detail. Today this area is a barren parking lot. *Yarmouth Portrait Co. photograph*

CLIFF STREET c. 1889

In this lovely view of Cliff Street looking west, five ladies in long skirts and fancy hats are out for an afternoon ride on their bicycles. At the end of Cliff Street, the Yarmouth Hotel on Main Street is shown, a building that still stands today. The cornerstone for St. John's Presbyterian Church was laid in 1873 and its spire was later removed in 1896. Today the shell of the church houses businesses—with the addition of modern siding.

COLLINS STREET

Looking west down Collins Street toward Yarmouth Harbour, it is easy to see why this area is considered one of the finest heritage districts in the province. The homes, built by wealthy merchants and sea captains, were built between 1875 and 1895. The Tabernacle Congregational Church, now the home of the Yarmouth County Museum, was built in 1892 and served its parish until 1967. This photograph is taken from a glass plate negative owned by Sandy Bain.

FOREST STREET, c. 1900

This view of the south side of Forest Street is representative of Yarmouth at the turn of the century. The house in the foreground was owned by merchant George Cann Lewis of the firm H & N. B. Lewis, shipowners, West India merchants and fishing outfitters. Lewis purchased the grand home on the death of George R. Smith in June 1898. Lewis died of tuberculosis in 1901 at the age of thirty-four. The middle house was built by Captain John E. Murphy upon his retirement from the sea c. 1885. Murphy was a highly respected master mariner, who later became the examiner at the Marine School. Murphy "dropped dead in the town" in 1925 at age seventy-nine and there were numerous accolades for him in the local papers. Asa Ellsworth McGray purchased the property for the furthest house in the photograph in 1883. McGray was a highly esteemed accountant and businessman, who held managerial positions with the Parker-Eakin's Company, the Yarmouth Steamship Company, and the Canadian Woodworking Company. McGray died in 1916 at the age of seventy-four.

JOHN STREET

This perfectly matched team was probably owned by James Bain who had boarding, hack, and livery stables on this stretch of John Street between Kirk and Willow. The early automobile alongside the horse and buggy illustrates the changing times. The building at the far end is still standing today as an apartment house; however, those in the foreground have given way to a Dairy Queen. *Parker photograph*

MAIN STREET SCENES

TOP RIGHT: At the corner of Collins and Main Streets, the wagon tracks on the road suggest activity in the street, depicting a typical busy scene in Yarmouth. McLaughlin Hall, owned by James and Daniel McLaughlin, opened in 1875 and was one of the finest examples of business architecture in the town. The company imported British and foreign dry goods and ready-made clothing, including a full line of American goods and English groceries. Competition was stiff, as next door Moses & Ross sold the same line of goods.

BOTTOM RIGHT: An interesting contrast in transportation modes lines Main Street at the corner of Lovitt. Curious, a customer has come out of the barber's chair to be included in the photograph. Hammocks and fancy baby carriages are displayed on the sidewalk. Behind the streetcar is the Scotia Lodge flag hanging from an upper window of the building. None of these buildings remain, and today modern retail businesses line the street at Lovitt Plaza.

THE CORNER OF COLLINS AND MAIN STREETS

THE CORNER OF LOVITT AND MAIN STREETS

MAIN STREET, 1858

Believed to be the earliest photograph of Yarmouth, this intriguing view of two little girls wandering along the main street is reproduced from a cracked, glass-covered daguerrotype owned by the National Archives of Canada. Believed to be taken in the vicinity of Cumberland Street, this image shows an interesting mix of residences and businesses.

MAIN STREET 1870

Looking north from Cliff Street, the R. H. Crocker store, in the foreground, was unique in the town for its decorative "false" front. Crocker was a merchant who also held shares in several Yarmouth vessels. His store was built after his first enterprise, located at the corner of Cliff and Main, burned down in 1868. The spire of the Cape Forchu Meeting House is visible in the background.

VANCOUVER STREET 1891

This 1891 photograph taken from "Mill Hill" at the corner of Grove Road shows the home of Hannah L. Burrell, widow of Joseph Burrell, one of the partners of the Burrell-Johnson Iron Company Foundry. This house later served as the nurses residence for the Yarmouth Hospital for many years. It was just recently torn down. The Town of Yarmouth can be seen across the water showing such landmarks as the Yarmouth Duck and Yarn Mill, the L. E. Baker homestead and several church spires. *Parker photograph*

WILLIAM STREET

WILLOW STREET

WILLIAM STREET

TOP LEFT: One of the loveliest streets in Yarmouth, William Street is admired for its Gothic architecture. Holy Trinity Church, built between 1868 and 1872, with its Gothic Revival attributes perhaps inspired the builders of the three gracious homes alongside it in this photograph. All three homes were built with the same layout; the "twin" homes in the foreground had more elaborate Gothic exteriors. These homes were built in the late 1870s and into the 1880s, at the height of Yarmouth's lucrative age of sail. Sadly, the first house in the foreground was destroyed by fire in 1992. How fortunate that the "twin" still stands in beautiful condition today.

WILLOW STREET

BOTTOM LEFT: Sunday afternoon brings families out to promenade on this quiet stretch of Willow Street at the corner of John Street. Bicycles, tricycles, wagons, and a tiller handle car add to the enjoyment. Every one of the nineteen people captured in this lovely photograph are wearing hats, as was fashionable for the times. The two homes shown are still in use today.

HIGHWAY 3 AT ARCADIA

The focal point of this photograph is the tidal Chebogue River which meanders down from the ocean throughout the settlement of Arcadia. The original English name of Upper Chebogue was changed to Arcadia in 1863. By the 1860s the village was thriving, with blacksmith shops, a grist mill, a tannery, a carriage-maker shop, a sawmill, and a cannery among others. The large building to the left of the river was built c. 1865 as a shoe factory and general store. The lower level stands today housing retail businesses. The building across from it, standing on stilts over the river, was built earlier in 1858 and was known as "Mechanics Hall." The home between the two buildings on the edge of the Kenny Hill Road was built in 1863 and stayed in the Allen family for several generations. It stands to this day in pristine condition in the heart of the village. *Believed to be a Parker photograph*

BEAVER RIVER CORNER

c. 1900

Beaver River was settled in the late 1700s by the industrious offspring of many of Yarmouth's first founding families; they were primarily farmers and foresters. In 1820 a huge fire ravaged the community destroying industries and barns; only three houses survived. On April 23, 1828, the first Temperance Society in British North America was founded in Beaver River. This photograph shows the Temperance Hall, which still stands today at the intersection.

CHEBOGUE ROAD

c. 1900

This farmhouse was built c. 1797 and was owned by James W. Killam from 1861 to 1910 when it was a show-place of the community. Killam was a wealthy farmer who supplied much of the meat, dairy products, and vegetables to local markets. Here Mr. and Mrs. Killam stand with friends and family in front of a fresh load of hay. The hay, drawn by a team of oxen, was transported along the Chebogue Road to the barn for winter fodder. The house still stands today.

HIGHWAY 1 AT HEBRON   In the early 1800s Anthony Landers built "Hebron House" near the junction of the Ohio and Main Roads. The community that later developed became known as Hebron. Visible in this photograph is the Faith United Church, built after a devastating fire levelled the original structure on December 7, 1890. The church was torn down in the early 1960s, and the congregation moved to the church at Milton.

HIGHWAY 1 AT DARLING LAKE

This community was named after Colonel Michael Ashley Darling in the 1790s, and was settled in the early 1800s by three Churchill brothers. A self-sustaining village, Darling Lake had a sluice, carding mill, sawmill, threshing mill, two shoe shops, a tannery, a blacksmith shop, and a way station. The Methodist church shown in the photograph was built in 1874 and was torn down in 1920 when its congregation merged with a neighbouring church. The village's most famous resident was Captain Aaron Flint Churchill, who was renowned for the "voyage of many rudders" and who built the imposing home, the Anchorage, known today as the Churchill Mansion. *Swain photograph*

Chapter 2

Domestic Architecture

RESIDENCE OF CAPTAIN JOHN KILLAM RYERSON

The captain built this magnificent $35,000 home on Parade Street in 1869, importing all the furnishings from England and France. At the time, it was considered one of the grandest homes in the province. Ryerson went to sea at an early age and rapidly rose to Master. Captain Ryerson was a successful businessman later in life as head of Ryerson, Moses & Co. He served as Yarmouth's elected representative to the first local Assembly formed after Confederation. He died December 19, 1890. In 1898 the home was purchased by the School Commissioners for $8,000 and it became the Yarmouth County Academy. On February 20, 1949, fire destroyed the building and the architectural legacy of Captain John Killam Ryerson. *Believed to be a Parker photograph*

BOARDING HOUSE

Mrs. Daniel Allen and daughter Winnifred are standing in front of the boarding house they ran on Kirk Street. This charming, asymmetrical home with its wooden walkway has since been replaced by Sentinel Printing.

RESIDENCE OF THE HONOURABLE STAYLEY BROWN

This lovely Italianate home was built in 1864 by a wealthy merchant with many Yarmouth shipping interests who was an outspoken opponent of Confederation. Brown served in the legislature for thirty-four years, was president of the Nova Scotia Executive Council, held the post of Receiver-General, and in 1875 became the provincial treasurer. By the 1990s this handsome home had been vacant for several years and had been damaged by a devastating fire. The house was saved from certain doom when it was purchased by the Dares family in 1995. Their labour of love restored this historic home to its original stately condition. In 1997 it was declared a Municipal *and* Provincial Heritage Property. The Brown home, now known as Harbour's Edge Bed and Breakfast, is once again a jewel of the town. *Swain photograph*

RESIDENCE OF THE HONOURABLE LORAN E. BAKER

This palatial home on Beacon Street belonged to Yarmouth's most prominent businessman and citizen throughout the late 1800s. Baker was a merchant, shipowner, entrepreneur, and legislative councillor, and has been credited with starting the tourist industry in Nova Scotia. The house became the Bethany Bible College, and was later demolished. It is now the site of Beacon United Church.

INTERIOR VIEW OF THE BAKER LIVING ROOM

In this striking example of Victorian living, one must surely question the safety of the draped fireplace. The large Japanese vase in the background is rare Kutaniware, and is one of a pair now proudly on display in the Yarmouth County Museum.

"Fir Banks" Exterior and Interior

TOP RIGHT: Situated on Vancouver Street was the magnificent home known as "Fir Banks" built by Robert Caie sometime after his marriage to Matilda Chandler in 1869. The home boasted spacious landscaped grounds, a circular drive, outbuildings, and an overflowing greenhouse. The house was ornate, down to small details such as decorative moldings and carvings over the windows and the gracefully curved dormers. The beautiful carved wood and stained glass area on the second floor was an addition to the house where another window had been. In the early 1960s this house, one of Yarmouth's finest examples of the high Victorian period, was demolished to make way for a more modern home. *Parker photograph*

BOTTOM RIGHT: This intriguing view at bottom right shows Mr. and Mrs. Robert Caie at home c. 1888 in their living room at "Fir Banks." The high ceiling, large draped windows, and all the Victorian accoutrements make this rare interior scene especially interesting. The quilted cat toy at Mr. Caie's feet is preserved in the collections of the Yarmouth County Museum.

BANK MANAGERS' RESIDENCE

This fine example of Queen Anne Revival style was built on Forest Street in 1903 for Thomas Van Buskirk Bingay, the first manager of the Yarmouth branch of the Bank of Montreal. Bingay sold the home to the bank ten days after he moved in and for eighty-one years it served as a residence for the bank's managers. The fine home is now a private residence. *Parker photograph*

"Fir Banks"

GEORGE GUEST HOUSE

RESIDENCE OF CAPTAIN BOWMAN CORNING

This house still stands today on Vancouver Street, although it is not easily recognized having lost all of the gingerbread, the summer kitchen, and the carriage house. This photograph shows Captain Corning standing at the gate of his beautiful home. His wife Mahalah Cann and daughter Mary Edna are seated on the front steps. Corning was a well-known commander in the mercantile navy and was for years associated with the Temperance cause. In 1860 a deadly epidemic took three of the Cornings' children within four days of one another. Daughter Mary Edna survived to wed Samuel A. Crowell, one of Yarmouth's wealthiest, self-made merchants.

RESIDENCE OF GEORGE AND MARY ELLEN GUEST

TOP LEFT: This unique Italianate home, the residence of George Guest and his wife Mary Ellen Lovitt was a wedding gift for the couple, built c. 1874 by Mary's father, the wealthy shipowner Captain John W. Lovitt. George Guest was also a shipowner and worked in the marine insurance business. In 1887 he became High Sheriff of Yarmouth County. The house stayed in the Lovitt/Guest family until 1924, after which it was home to several families. Although today the cupola is gone this beautiful home is an enduring reminder of Yarmouth's "golden age of sail."

BACKYARDS ALONG SEMINARY STREET

This unusual view illustrates that in the Victorian era as much care was given to designing backyards as was given to designing homes. This photograph shows the backyards of houses on Seminary Street as seen from Pleasant Street. From left to right are the homes of Captain Byron A. Abbott, master mariner; Abel Cutler Robbins, shipowner; James E. Clements, bookkeeper for the Yarmouth Steamship Company. Central School is visible behind the Clements' house. The Robbins' yard was truly a masterpiece design with its elaborate greenhouse, terraced lawns, rock fountain, archways, twig furniture, and the wonderful carriage house. The carriage house stood until only a few years ago when it had to be torn down. The beautiful Second Empire style house was damaged by two fires over several years and completely lost in 1997.

PELTON-FULLER HOUSE

This lovely home was built between 1890 and 1895 by Edward B. Cann, a well-known merchant who operated a successful clothing store at the corner of Main and Central Streets. The home was later owned by the Bown and Pelton family but is more well known as the summer home of Primrose (Pelton) & Alfred Fuller—the Annapolis Valley native who started the Fuller Brush Company. In 1996 this home and its contents were donated to the Yarmouth County Historical Society. Today it is operated as a seasonal heritage home exhibit—focusing on the Pelton and Fuller families and the Fuller Brush Company.

JOHN MURRAY LAWSON RESIDENCE

TOP RIGHT: This house, built c. 1898 with intriguing nautical flare, is situated on William Street. The Lawson name was associated with journalism in Yarmouth for nearly ninety-two years. J. Murray's father, Alexander, moved to Yarmouth in 1833 and in August of that year established the Yarmouth Herald, thus beginning Yarmouth's heritage of newspaper excellence. Young Murray entered his father's employ as a youth and started at the bottom. Proving himself to be an excellent newspaperman, he assumed proprietorship and the editorial chair upon his father's death in 1895, a position J. Murray held for thirty years, until his own death in 1925. The Lawson legacy of journalism has served Yarmouth well. Today the newspapers and reference works compiled by J. Murray, form the cornerstone of the Yarmouth County Museum Archives and are used by researchers on a daily basis. *Believed to be a Parker photograph*

GOTHIC REVIVAL ARCHITECTURE

BOTTOM RIGHT: This imposing home was built c. 1864 by William Dodge Lovitt, grandson of Andrew Lovitt, one of the early grantees of the town. William was one of Yarmouth's leading shipowners from 1858 to 1894. As well, he was one of the founders of the Yarmouth Water Company, the first president of the Yarmouth Duck & Yarn Company, a member of nearly all the organizations in the town and a generous, community-minded citizen. The house was eventually moved back from the street. Today it is part of the Lakelawn Motel on Main Street at Milton.

JOHN MURRAY LAWSON RESIDENCE

GOTHIC REVIVAL ARCHITECTURE

New England Colonial Style House

Residence of Judge Murray

NEW ENGLAND COLONIAL STYLE HOME

TOP LEFT: This house was built c. 1819 by Robert Black. The two-storey addition with Victorian influences is thought to have been added by John Wentworth Moody in the late 1800s. Although the house is asymmetrical, the balance achieved by the two sections is pleasing to the eye. The house has had several owners whose occupations have included trader, merchant, mariner, railway locomotive engineer, and "esquire." Standing today on Main Street South, the "Moody Home" is still a prominent part of the streetscape.

RESIDENCE OF JUDGE J. MURRAY

BOTTOM LEFT: Judge James Murray receives afternoon guests at his front gate at the corner of Main and Forest Streets. The fancy dress, sleeping dog, and fine black riding horse are noteworthy details. The impressive Regency style house has Gothic influences and was built c. 1820–25. It was a gift from the Honourable James Bond to his daughter Anne and her husband James Murray, Judge of the Probate Court. Judge Murray died October 31, 1898, but the home stayed in the family until 1936. Today the home, Murray Manor, is a Bed and Breakfast, known for its lovely gardens and original stone wall built over 150 years ago.

RESIDENCE OF THE HONOURABLE EDGAR KEITH SPINNEY

Influenced by Second Empire style, this house was located on the corner of Main and Glebe Streets in the heart of town. The c. 1890s photograph has many interesting details: the group gathered at the front gate, trained ivy, lush gardens, and the canary in the second-storey window. Spinney was a self-made merchant who established his first business at the age of twenty-two. He was a Member of the Union Government, sat on several town boards, and conducted business in the United Kingdom, Europe, and North America. At the time of his death in 1926, his company, E. K. Spinney Limited, had been one of the leading mercantile establishments in the Maritimes for over fifty years. The two levels of the original house were incorporated into the present-day building which now houses the offices of the L. G. Trask Agency Ltd. Yarmouth's new Town Hall has in recent years replaced the house visible on the far right.

LEVI B. WYMAN HOME

Built in 1892, this house was said to be "the finest piece of architecture of this class to be found in the Maritime Provinces." A magnificent example of Queen Anne Revival architecture, it was built on a sweeping lot on the corner of Park and Cliff Streets. Wyman was born in Yarmouth in 1847 and was actually a blacksmith by trade. In April 1868 he travelled to California—along with several other Yarmouthians—lured by the possibilities of the Gold Rush. Arriving back in 1874 Wyman established his first grocery business and conducted an obviously successful trade. In 1954 the home was purchased by the Roman Catholic Episcopal Corporation and has been used for the residence of the Bishop ever since. *Believed to be a Parker photograph*

Chapter 3

Businesses

J. W. GRANT & CO.

The owner, J. W. Grant, was mayor of Yarmouth from 1917–18. Located at the corner of Brown and Hawthorne, the company was later sold to the Yarmouth Fruit Company. Shown in front of the building are Lyman Cleveland, Monde Amirault, J. W. Grant, and George Atkins.

WILLIAM LAW & CO.

The business was started by William Law, who was joined by his son Bowman. William Law was active in the business community, having been a shipowner and agent for the Boston Marine Insurance Company. Bowman B. Law was the well-known MP for Yarmouth who died in the Parliament Building fire in 1916.

NICKERSON'S BARBER SHOP The barber shop, owned by Keith Nickerson, was established in 1911. Shown are brothers John and Keith Nickerson with staff and clients.

BOWERS' CAFÉ

This charming café was located on Main Street between Cliff and John Streets. Owned by Addison J. Bower and his wife Annie, the café was a restaurant and ice cream parlour. Addison, a former sailor, was a successful businessman who also ran a retail piano shop.

PEOPLE'S MEAT & FISH MARKET

This hard-working butcher wears sleeve guards to protect his shirt. Fresh sausage and meat quarters fill the store, which was located on Main Street.

McLaughlin Bros.

This business, located on the corner of Main and Collins Streets, operated from 1875 to 1932. McLaughlin Bros. dealt in watches, clocks, silverware, diamonds, opticals, and optical supplies. The street level portion of this building still stands today and houses City Drug.

E. J. Vickery Bookseller & Stationer

RIGHT: This well-known Main Street shop—photographed in 1895, ten years after the business opened—boasted a large assortment of books and a circulating library. It was located opposite the Post Office. Its interior view (bottom oval) suggests the business carried a wide selection of its specialty.

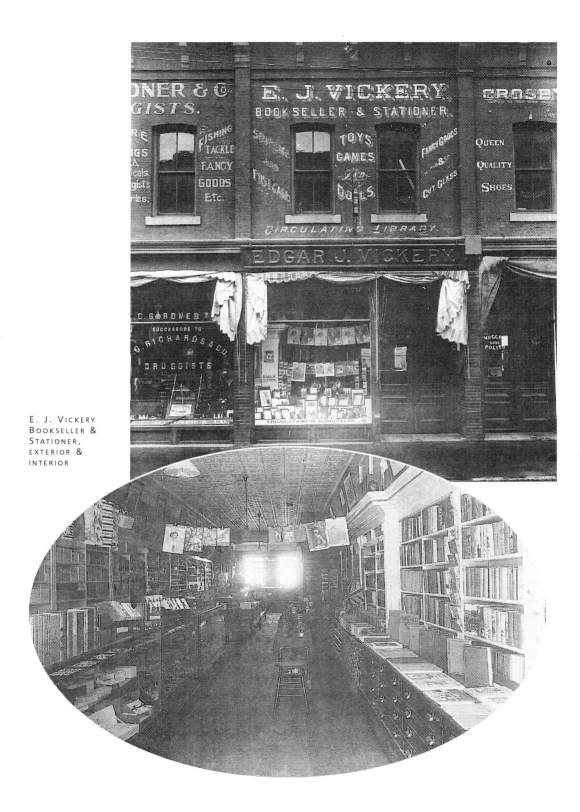

E. J. Vickery
Bookseller &
Stationer,
exterior &
interior

YARMOUTH CYCLE CO. 1900

cycles Landing at Yarmouth Cycle Co.

Stock of over 150 bicycles arrives for sale. This company was established in 1894 by Frank C. Robbins. By 1900 it was the largest distributor of bicycles and accessories in Eastern Canada. Later it was renamed the Yarmouth Cycle & Motor Co.

YARMOUTH CIGAR CO.

L. J. Roy's cigar factory on Brown Street produced the "Yarmouth Beauty." All the cigars were painstakingly rolled by hand. L. J. Roy, Sr. is shown standing with his hands in pockets, while his son, L. J. Roy, Jr. is seated far right, facing the camera.

JAMES ROZEE, WHOLESALE & RETAIL CONFECTIONER

James Rozee, shown centre, operated this business that included an ice cream shop with a seating area at the rear. An example of the interesting tin ceilings of the day is visible here.

KEMPTVILLE LUMBER MANU-FACTURING COMPANY

The village of Kemptville, named for the provincial governor of the day, was settled in 1820. Due to the heavy-growth forests of the region, several sawmills were established. Oxen played a major role in getting the lumber to market due to the outlying location of the village. This particular mill had a very short life. It began operation in 1888, and despite the company's energetic approach, quick expansion coupled with a business recession caused its demise in 1899.

THE OVERTON LAUNDRY

The community of Overton lies on the west side of Yarmouth Harbour, having been named for its location "over town." Although primarily a small farming and fishing community, by the turn of the century the area also boasted two popular hotels, the Markland and the Bayview. The little cottage industry grew out of the need for fresh laundry for visitors, usually Americans who had travelled on one of the Boston ferries. The gentleman holding the basket is Wilbur McGray.

DICKIE & MACGRATH MILL

This prosperous mill was located on the Tusket River, in the heart of the village of the same name. The eighty-foot chimney belonged to an earlier mill located on the same site. At its peak the mill employed approximately two hundred people but that number would dwindle drastically during haying season when men were needed to work in the fields. The schooner, with its unusual clipper bow, is probably taking on milled wood for the West Indies. The two tugs would have assisted the empty barge to dock. *Parker photograph, c. 1915.*

Yarmouth Brass Foundry

This foundry advertised "Particular attention paid to Vessels' Fastenings and Fittings." The company was located on Water Street and was operated by Pendrigh & Crawford.

W. H. Gridley Ship Smith

Located on Water Street near the foot of Brown Street, W. H. Gridley Ship Smith forged anchors, tillers, and such items for many of Yarmouth's ships. Here, a blacksmith stands next to forged anchors.

COSMOS COTTON COMPANY

DRYER FELT
LOOMS, ABOVE,
AND SPINNING
ROOM, RIGHT

Workers run the dryer felt looms (top) at Cosmos Cotton Company located on Water Street, c. 1920. Cosmos Cotton took over from the Yarmouth Duck & Yarn Co. Ltd. in 1902, and operated until 1926 when it was sold to Cosmos Imperial Mills. In 1973 Dominion Textile Inc. took over from Cosmos and operated the "cotton mill" until 1991 when the plant was closed. From its founding in 1883, until its devastating closure in 1991, the "cotton mill" was Yarmouth's primary large-scale industry for 108 years.

YARMOUTH WOOLEN MILLS AND DYE WORKS

Erected in 1881, this mill was enlarged shortly thereafter in 1895. By 1918 the building had been converted to house the Yarmouth Cold Storage Company plant. *Swain photograph*

MILTON IRON FOUNDRY

This photograph of the Milton Foundry was taken during Frank H. Wilson's proprietorship. Located in the North end of Yarmouth and established in 1871, this company manufactured stoves, ranges, (wood & coal) and so on for the home or ships.

KILLAM BROTHERS

This building, located on Yarmouth's waterfront, is considered to be the oldest shipping office in Canada. Built c. 1835, the Killam family's businesses included shipping and a coal operation. Only the front portion of the building remains today, part of which is operated as a seasonal museum.

PARKER-EAKIN'S WHARF

TOP RIGHT: The Parker-Eakin's & Co. office staff, c. 1900, is shown in the oval photograph. Established in 1874, this company once had one of the largest businesses in Nova Scotia. Business interests included commission merchants, wholesale grocers, and fish exports. As well, they were feed merchants and wholesale lumber dealers. In later days, they sold hardware.

BOTTOM RIGHT: Parker-Eakin's was so successful at marketing fish flakes (salted cod) that the food became known as "Nova Scotia turkey." The company's sail loft is shown at right and "Pinky" *Eva V* is at the dock.

TREFRY'S GARAGE   In 1917 Trefry's Garage, dealers of Ford and Studebakers, was considered the largest and most modern garage in the Maritimes. Trefry also operated a livery and automobile cab service.

GRAND HOTEL c. 1917

As viewed from Victoria Park, the three-storey brick building with mansard roof was opened in 1894 with electric lighting. It is believed the writer Meredith Wilson wrote the well-known Christmas carol, "It's Beginning to Look a lot Like Christmas" while staying there. The building was razed in 1966 for construction of a modern facility. *Believed to be a Parker photograph*

LORNE HOTEL

Originally the residence of S. A. Ryerson, located on Main Street, across from Brown Street, the building was raised two floors and opened as a hotel in 1879 by Mrs. D. McIntosh of Kentville. Full service included use of a livery stable accessed from the hotel front. It later became the site of the Capital, then Odeon theatres. *Swain photograph*

Located in Dayton on Lake Milo, the inn was built by Canadian Pacific Hotels and featured sixty-eight rooms and five cottages. In its heyday the hotel held a five-star rating and was an equally popular destination for visiting Americans and locals. The building currently serves as St. Joseph's Villa Du Lac nursing home.

Chapter 4

Public *Architecture*

WESTERN COUNTIES RAILWAY STATION

The George B. Doane locomotive stops at the Western Counties
Railway Station located on Water Street. The station was built in 1879.
In 1894 the Windsor and Annapolis Railway purchased the railway
tracks, naming the new line the Dominion Atlantic Railway (D. A. R.).
A Tim Horton's/Wendy's restaurant is now at this site; the building was
designed to resemble the original train station.
Alfred S. Hood photograph, c. 1880

The community of Canaan is located on the south side of Mill Lake, on the
Tusket River system. During the early twentieth century, this community lost
several of its schools to fire. The school pictured here burned about 1908; the
one that replaced it in 1910 was also destroyed by fire the following year.

CENTRAL
SCHOOL

Also called the Yarmouth Seminary, the building was completed in 1864 and was
principally a gift of George Killam. The schoolgrounds covered almost three
acres. Today the site holds a more modern brick elementary school, also called
Central School. In this photograph the girls are playing croquet, the boys are
playing cricket. The house on Seminary Street in the background still stands and
is the home of Juniper House. *Swain photograph*

SALEM SCHOOL

The Salem area of Yarmouth was formally called Broad Brook Settlement. About the time of this photograph, a town school trustees' census showed a population of 228 with an average school attendance of 34. This now demolished schoolhouse was photographed in 1890. *Parker photograph*

OLD MILTON LIBRARY

Located on Main Street, this Gothic Revival style building was constructed in 1888 to house the Milton Library. The land was donated by Charles E. Brown and the building by Mrs. Robert Caie and Miss Clara Killam. In 1958 the building became home to the Yarmouth County Museum. Today it is the site of the Lighthouse Baptist Church.

St. John's Presbyterian Church, c. 1890

RIGHT: Located on the corner of Kirk and Cliff Streets, this building's cornerstone was laid in 1873 on the site of a previous church that had been moved across the street. The Romanesque style building still stands today but no longer features the same architectural attributes.

Tabernacle Congregational Church

BELOW: The cornerstone of this church on Collins Street was laid in 1892 and a dedication service was held in August 1893. This building, constructed of Shelburne granite, was built to replace its Main Street predecessor that had been destroyed by fire. After the formation of the United Church of Canada the name changed to Central United Church. Since 1967 the building has provided a unique setting for the Yarmouth County Museum and Archives.
Yarmouth Portrait Co. Photograph, c. 1920

CAPE FORCHU MEETING HOUSE

RIGHT: This church, the predecessor of Zion, was opened for worship in 1841 but had been in construction since July 1784. It is recorded that the windows were not added until 1790, and it was without seats and a pulpit for some time. It was located on Main Street, near where the cenotaph now stands. The original Grand Hotel can be seen in the background. *Parker photograph, c. 1895*

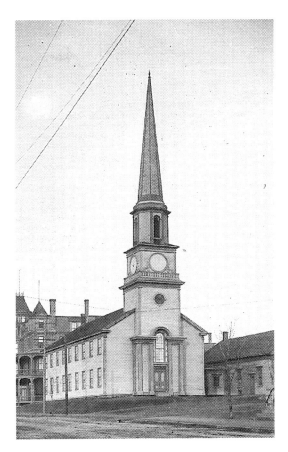

ZION UNITED BAPTIST CHURCH

BELOW: This photo, taken July 1895, shows the laying of the cornerstone for what is now called Zion United Baptist Church (formerly called the First Baptist Church). Located on Parade Street, this church was built to replace the church on Main Street. The dedication of this church took place on June 7, 1896. This photo is noted as showing "Grandpa Smith," but it is unknown which individual he is.

STE. ANNE'S CHURCH

SOUTH OHIO CHURCH

STE. ANNE'S CHURCH

TOP LEFT: This church is located in the community of Ste. Anne du Ruisseau, commonly known as Eel Brook because of its Indian name Wipkoogmajokun, meaning "place for eels." The community is the oldest Catholic Parish in Yarmouth County, founded in 1799. This Romanesque style church—built in 1901 after the previous one burned in 1900—is the only municipally registered Catholic Church in the county.

SOUTH OHIO CHURCH, c. 1900

BOTTOM LEFT: Built in 1852, this church still stands in the fork of the road at South Ohio, part of the original area named Ohio by brothers Nehemiah and Benjamin Churchill. The church sustained damage to its spire and tower in 1917 after lightning struck it. Those sections were never restored to their original form.

HOLY TRINITY CHURCH, c. 1875

At the time of this photo William Street not only featured impressive architecture like this Gothic Revival church, but also farmland. Holy Trinity Church was opened in 1872. By 1913 its spire was removed. The house shown is on the corner of Forest Street and is currently the residence of the church's minister. Holy Trinity is noted for its stained glass windows.
Swain photograph

THE PHOENIX RINK

YARMOUTH MUNICIPAL HOME AT ARCADIA

THE PHOENIX RINK 1882

TOP LEFT: Better known as the exhibition building, this structure was built c. 1878 as the Yarmouth Skating Rink. Early one morning in June 1893, fire destroyed the building which at the time contained the Agricultural Society's material for their annual exhibition. *Swain photograph*

YARMOUTH MUNICIPAL HOME AT ARCADIA

BOTTOM LEFT: This landmark three-storey Georgian style home was built in 1870 as the Municipal Home for the poor. It was a working farm which was mostly self-sustaining. Over the years the home has been called the Poor's Asylum and later the Riverview Home. In 1975 residents were moved to Harbourside Lodge at the Yarmouth Hospital, and the home was closed. In March 1997 this building was demolished. On July 1, 1997, the unmarked burial ground for the home was declared an Historic Site by the Yarmouth County Historical Society.

OPERATING ROOM AT OLD YARMOUTH HOSPITAL

Sparsely furnished, this Old Yarmouth Hospital operating room appears questionably equipped by today's standards. It was located in the south end of town on the corner of Church and Sycamore Streets. The building was donated to the hospital society by Jacob Bingay (shipowner) in 1911 and served as such until 1918 when the hospital was moved to Vancouver Street. This south end building, built c. 1843, is currently a private residence, which was just recently registered as a Municipal Heritage Property.

SOUTH END FIRE ENGINE HOUSE

St. George Co. No. 1 Engine House was located in the south end of town. Built in 1899 to replace a previous engine house that burned, the building was used until 1975, when the various town fire departments moved to the new Pleasant Street Fire Hall. The engine house shown here was destroyed by fire on January 18, 1991, at which time it was used as a storage building for Munroe's Furniture.

MILTON FIRE ENGINE HOUSE

Naiad Co. No. 2 Engine House, built in 1860, was located in the north end of town where Milton Ball Park is today. In 1862 this building was moved across the street, but it does not exist today. This building was similar to the previous home of the Naiad Co., originally located on Vancouver Street on the other side of Milton Dam. Milton School can be seen in the background, dating this photograph to between 1860 and 1862.

POST OFFICE

This three-storey structure housed the Post Office and Customs Office. Built in 1886 it featured a clock tower with six-foot clock faces that can still be seen in the clock tower of the Town Hall building. The post office building was torn down in 1959. Located on the corner of John and Main Streets, it is the current location of the Canadian Imperial Bank of Commerce.

COURTHOUSE DURING LORD ABERDEEN'S VISIT Taken on August 27, 1894, this photo shows the Courthouse decorated for a reception in honour of the visit of Lord and Lady Aberdeen. The governor general and his wife visited Yarmouth by train and stayed next to the Courthouse at the Grand Hotel. Lord Aberdeen presided over the Dominion from 1893 until he was succeeded by the Earl of Minto in 1898.

OLD YARMOUTH LIGHT AT CAPE FORCHU

Shown is the Old Yarmouth Lighthouse and keeper's dwelling house located at Cape Forchu. The lighthouse was put into operation on January 15, 1840, and remained until December 1961 when it was replaced by a concrete tower. This first light was a sixty-four foot cone-shaped wooden building.

Chapter 5

Special Events, Sports & Leisure

PATRIOTIC FUND PAGEANT

Year after year, American visitors spent the summer months in Yarmouth. In this photograph, one such visitor, whose name was not recorded, organized this local Patriotic Fund Pageant in August 1916. Participants put on skits, danced and entertained the audience, while everyone enjoyed local delicacies of chowder and blueberry pie on the shores of Lake Milo. Frances Goudey is the young lady with the dark hair and flower at her ear.

Special Events

LORD ABERDEEN'S VISIT TO YARMOUTH

On August 27, 1895, Governor General Lord and Lady Aberdeen arrived at the Yarmouth train station where they were greeted by various officials and a large group of curious citizens. They were then paraded along Main Street to the Grand Hotel in a torchlight procession headed by the Yarmouth Brass Band and the Yarmouth Garrison Artillery. This photograph shows the Grand Hotel decorated for the occasion and some of the throngs—including people on the roof of the hotel—awaiting the arrival of the guests of honour.

I.O.D.E. EXHIBITION OF WAR "TROPHIES"

The Markland Chapter of the Imperial Order Daughters of the Empire was founded October 1, 1917, when twenty-nine members met and enrolled at the home of Mrs. G. W. T. Farish. With the motto "Loyal In Everything," the ladies set out to do civic-minded work, helping in many ways with the war effort. This photograph, taken between 1917 and 1925, shows a rather bizarre collection of war trophies brought back by Yarmouth soldiers from the Great War. The uniform hanging on the line suggests the injury its wearer must have suffered.

RETURN FROM THE BOER WAR

L. Wolseley Bingay's triumphant return from the Boer War on September 27, 1900, was cause for great celebration in Yarmouth. Main Street was festooned with flags, and bunting hung from all parts of town. Private Bingay was greeted at the train station by the mayor and other officials. With the Yarmouth Brass Band in the lead, a happy crowd proceeded along Main Street to the Courthouse, where Bingay was presented with a purse of gold in the amount of $265.

Note the Yarmouth Garrison Artillery members wearing "pill box" hats, to the right of Bingay. (See also the photograph of Bingay and Tooker "Photographers and their Subjects," pages 103–115.)

The laying of the first water pipe was a significant event because it brought fresh water from Lake George in the community of Brenton into the town of Yarmouth. The pipes were imported from Glasgow, and the first section was laid on June 1, 1881. The last pipe was laid on Saturday November 19, 1881. On December 8 the taps in town were turned on for the first time. Shown here are Mr. and Mrs. Comfort Clements and their children, Judson and Etta along with several workers.

Here the station at Pubnico celebrates its opening on July 29, 1897. The Coast Railway ran from Yarmouth to Lockeport, later connecting with the Halifax line, successfully linking the small and picturesque villages along the south coast of Nova Scotia. Designed to complement the Boston ferry service, the railway service was heavily promoted to American tourists as a vacation of rest and relaxation.

Sports

VICTORIA CYCLING CLUB, c. 1893

These three young men are proudly showing off their cycling gear in an unknown photographer's studio. They shared their home track, Victoria Park, with sulky horses. The man to the left is George Earle.

VICTORIA PARK RACETRACK

Built at the corner of Cottage Street and Starrs Road—the present site of the Yarmouth Exhibition Grounds—the track was used not only by sulky racers, but also by the members of the Victoria Park Cycling Club. Later the track was modified to suit motor car racing. Yarmouth no longer has a track at all.

GYM CLASS

This photograph shows a rare glimpse of Evelina Patten's girls' gymnastics class in September 1893. The group met at the Oddfellows Building on the corner of Second and John Streets. Using Indian clubs and balance weights, the young women sought to improve their strength and posture under the careful guidance of their instructor.

YARMOUTH HOCKEY CLUB 1901

This photograph shows the Yarmouth Hockey Club one year after its founding in December 1900. Back row: Joseph R. Wyman, Harry Munro, Bud Moody; Middle Row: Roy Wyman, Bert Perry, Clem Cann, Horace Porter, Prescott Baker; Front Row: Errol Hogan, Hal Cann, Israel Porter, Bill McLaughlin, Chas. Tooker.

YARMOUTH TENNIS CLUB

Located on the lawn behind Holy Trinity Church on William Street, tennis was a favourite pastime of many Yarmouthians; the sport was popular with both men and women. This photograph, taken c. 1900, shows entire families out for the afternoon. One can only imagine how difficult it must have been for ladies to serve the ball while wearing their long dresses with cinched waists. A clubhouse was eventually built at a cost of $1,000 by selling shares to the club's members.

YARMOUTH GATEWAYS, NOVA SCOTIA CHAMPIONS 1934

Yarmouth has a great sports heritage; the love of baseball lives on to this day. The Yarmouth Gateways was our greatest team, capturing provincial titles in 1929, 1932, 1934, and 1937. Crowds of well over one thousand people regularly supported the team, and most of the local businesses would close during the ball games. So keen was the interest that inning by inning results were passed to the local telegraph office and posted on billboards throughout the town. Pitcher Nate Bain and the 1929 and 1935 Gateways teams were inducted into the Nova Scotia Sports Heritage Hall of Fame in 1981.

Leisure

ON THE SEA

Many of Yarmouth's leisure activities took place on the water or next to the water. In this photo the Haskell Brothers have organized their annual community boat race off Port Maitland, which in 1908 was well attended.

FAMILY PICNIC

Sunday was visiting day, and here the Patten family has gathered for a family picnic "across the pond at the old Patten homestead." This charming photograph was taken by Enos Parker on August 22, 1901, in the area now known as the Tin Pot Road section of Lake Milo—Lake Milo is the "pond" referred to on the reverse of the original photograph. The children's elaborate clothing is particularly interesting.

Mr. and Mrs. John H. Killam are entertaining friends and family c. 1898 at their cottage on Lake Annis. John Killam was one of the original founders of Killam Brothers, one of Yarmouth's most important and long-standing businesses. In this photograph Mr. Killam is to the far right, Mrs. Killam is in the front row centre. Some of their guests include Mrs. Charles Brown, Mrs. E. H. Armstrong, Mrs. E. J. Vickery, Mrs. Burrill, and Mrs. Kelley. Two of the Killam's daughters, Nellie and Mabel are also present. This whimsical photograph captures the cottage lifestyle: porch hammocks, picnic basket, children, and sun hats. Even cottage humour is present in the two unidentified guests in costume. *Parker photograph*

**ON THE
ISLANDS**

Going "to the islands" is an enjoyable tradition in Yarmouth County. This photograph, taken July 23, 1891, on Peases Island, is one in a series with the preceding photographs: "Landed—Last Boat Load," and "Expectation—The Chowder Cooking." This photo is titled "Realization—Eating the Chowder," while the last photo is captioned "Satisfaction—The Chowder Eaten." This photograph comes from the incredible Laura Lawson album, and the party is likely a group of visiting journalists. *Believed to be a Parker photograph*

ON THE SHORE

The Yarmouth Yacht Club, situated in Yarmouth Harbour, was organized on January 16, 1895, and provided a venue not only for pleasure boating, but also for the competitive races for which it became famous. The clubhouse shown here was built in 1896, when an impressive silver cup was awarded to the competitor who won the cup race three times in succession. The Yacht Club is gone but the race has been resurrected and renamed the Yarmouth Cup Ocean Race. The name of the winner of the 174-nautical mile ocean race between Falmouth, Maine, and Yarmouth is placed on the original cup.

AT THE FISHING HOLE

This tranquil scene is titled "L. Campbell Mill, Mr. and Mrs. Morton fishing on the Tusket River." It is not known where the Campbell Mill was on the Tusket River, although it is possible that it was in Kemptville, an area known for its mills and Morton families. The woman to the far left has immersed her bare feet in the water.

This snapshot taken in July 1912 at Deerfield, Yarmouth County epitomizes leisure time. The inscription on the reverse suggests that Uncle Moses is telling Charlie and Fernald Allen the story of "Lucifer." The open back door gives us a glimpse inside of Uncle Moses' house, showing a cot under the window and the table set with a white cloth.

Chapter 6

Uniforms

THE CRASH OF AIRCRAFT NO. 9039

About to perform a flypast during the service at the Yarmouth cenotaph on November 11, 1941, this aircraft lost power on takeoff and its propellers touched the runway. Fortunately, the pilot was able to regain airspeed and circled the airport several times, dumping extra fuel before making a belly landing on the grass. No one was injured. Left to right in the photograph are Sergeant Bill Howes, pilot; Sergeant Game, wireless operator; and Corporal Bill Mart.

Military

FOUR MEMBERS OF THE YARMOUTH MILITIA,
c. 1884

These four members of the Yarmouth Battalion Garrison Artillery (Militia), are in their dress uniforms, and judging from the pipe-clayed belts and shoulder sashes, polished belt buckles and shoes, they are ready for inspection. The young man at bottom centre is "Corn" Webster, who in an 1886 photograph is a corporal and in one taken in 1887, is shown wearing sergeant's stripes.
Parker Studio photograph

MEMBERS OF THE YARMOUTH ARTILLERY,
c.1900

At least thirty-four men are on parade here; their officer, Lieutenant Tom Seeley, is at right. This picture was taken on Main St. at the foot of John Street, some fifty yards away was their John Street Drill Hall.

THE BOYS BRIGADE

1901

This group of young lads surround their leader under the gaze of Queen Victoria and her son, soon to become King Edward VII. The Boys Brigade was a youth organization operated on military lines of the day and stressed the qualities of devotion to one's country, good conduct, and self-discipline. Their drill muskets are three-quarter size carbines made with wooden barrels to prevent injury.

RECRUITS AT THE D.A.R. STATION

NOV. 9, 1914

Most of these young men were leaving to serve their country in an adventure they would always remember—if they returned. In this group are George Meisner, Bishara (with cigar), John Nichols, Bob Clements, Don Chipman, and Arthur Hood.

JACK McMULLEN, LITTLE SOLDIER

Jack McMullen, wearing sergeant's stripes and carrying his swagger stick, is ready to take on the Huns during the First World War. These well-tailored little suits were available by catalogue from Eaton's so youngsters could dress like their older brothers and fathers who were leaving for or were already at "the front."

A RECRUITING DRIVE

Taken on July 30, 1915, these young recruits are part of a parade driving through Yarmouth. They are carrying a placard which reads [We have] "Enlisted to go with Machine Gun (Corps). Who will be the next."

In this photograph of a recruiting parade on Main Street in Yarmouth, several members of the SS *Prince George*, in their uniforms surround a banner which reads: "The SS *Prince George* has 12 men At The Front." Below this a large placard with a picture of the German Kaiser is titled "We Will Get Him Yet." (The *Prince George* was one of the Yarmouth to Boston steamers which went away on war service with the British Admiralty.)

**MACHINE
GUN
SECTION
112TH
OVERSEAS
BATTALION**

The Machine Gun Section of the 112th Overseas Battalion are shown with their Lewis light machine guns before they embarked for Europe. Sent as a postcard to Dennis Amireau of Yarmouth, the message read in part: "I just came from the hospital yesterday, and we are going tomorrow … Kiss Hilda for me and [tell her] [it] will be a long time before she will see Papa again. From A. M. D." It was mailed from Windsor, Nova Scotia, on July 22. Did he return? *Photograph by "Palmers Studio"*

Maynard B. Wyman (standing) and Wilfred Adolphus Wyman were Yarmouth brothers who served their country in the Great War. Maynard is shown here in his Nova Scotia Highland Brigade walking out uniform; Wilfred's "hospital uniform" was worn while he was recovering from wounds received as a member of the 25th Battalion, Canadian Expeditionary Force. The Yarmouth County Museum Archives contains a vast series of letters which Wilfred wrote between the day he left home until the day he was killed in action on November 6, 1918, while serving with the 25th Battn., an especially aggressive unit in the field.

PARADING ALONG MAIN ST. Led by the drum and bugle band, RCAF Station Yarmouth parades along Main Street in the early 1940s. This station was part of Coastal Command, which kept careful watch for enemy submarines in our coastal waters.

The navy came to Yarmouth during the Second World War as part of the
Commonwealth Air Training Plan. "East Camp" on the eastern side of the
airport was a training base for the Royal Navy's Fleet Air Arm Telegraphist Air
Gunners. Servicemen from various countries served here and many of them
married local girls and settled in Yarmouth. In this photograph several sailors are
enjoying tea in the home of Miss Eakins who lived in one of the Gothic style
houses on William Street.

The Second World War was financed by War Bonds and Loans as well as taxes.
Factories, schools, banks, and social "Booster" Clubs held challenges to raise
funds. This photograph, taken outside the Headquarters Building at RCAF
Station Yarmouth, shows that the nationwide challenge of raising $70,000 for the
5th Victory Loan had been exceeded, and that with the help of small loans across
Canada $87,500 had been raised.

Bands

The Yarmouth Concert Band, formed in 1927 under the leadership of Laurie Smith, had no uniforms so to get them they joined the local militia en masse in 1932 as the 84th Battery Band. The bandmaster was Penn Spicer, seated below the middle of the door with S. C. Hood, the militia battery commander, on his left. This photograph was taken in front of the Exhibition building, probably in the early 1930s.

MILTON
BRASS
BAND

Milton forms the northern portion of Yarmouth and was in the early days almost a separate town. The Milton Brass Band is shown here in 1875 in their new uniforms aboard the "band wagon," which was built in 1875 at the cost of $500. The band wagon was used until at least 1917 for the band as well as for picnics, and was converted to a sleigh in the wintertime. It was lost when fire consumed the stable where it was housed.

Miscellaneous Uniforms

JIM MACMULLEN, POLICEMAN

Born in Cardiff, Wales, Jim MacMullen was a Yarmouth police officer, a private officer for the Eastern Steamship Company, and a provincial police officer.

LADIES ON PARADE

Are these theatrical or genuine uniforms? Taken c. 1895, this photograph illustrates a group of young ladies known as the "Red Hussars." Left to right they are: Mary/Marie Guest (Tooker), Helen Cann (Pope), May Crowell, Jean Grant (Hood), Alice Cary/Violet Paliver, Bessie Paliver/Violet Paliver, Addie Richards, Sadie Kirk, Ada Platt, Maude/Edna Wyman, Alva Bain/Mrs. H. G. Perry with Carrie Campbell behind holding the flags. *Enos Parker photograph*

OFFICERS AND CREW OF SS *BOSTON*   Probably taken in Boston in the early 1900s when the *Boston* was part of the Dominion Atlantic Railway (D. A. R.) fleet, this photograph shows Captain William McKenzie (seated in the front row, wearing the white "Edward VII" style goatee) with his officers and crew.

Chapter 7

Shipping

LIFE AT SEA ON THE *GENELVAN*

Captain Evelyn E. Robbins is shown posed on the deck of his ship,
the *Genelvan*, in Tacoma, Washington, in 1898. The photographer,
William Hester, specialized in photographs of ships and their crews
visiting the various Puget Sound ports. Built in Glasgow, Scotland,
in 1895 the vessel would have been in Tacoma to load either grain or
wood. Captain Robbins is shown, telescope in hand, in his best set of
shore-going clothes.

Yarmouth Ships

SHIP LILLIE SOULLARD

Built in 1871 in Port Gilbert, Nova Scotia, the *Lillie Soullard* was named after the wife of a Savannah, Georgia, ship agent. After twenty years of good service to Yarmouth owners the ship was sold to Saint John interests for $4,000 and was renamed *Lockwood.* This photograph shows her secured to one of Yarmouth's many wharves. The crew, all facing the camera, were aware this picture was being taken, as was the captain and his wife sitting on the cabin top with their children or some female visitors. *Swain photograph*

SHIP *RUBY* AT TUSKET WEDGE

TOP RIGHT: The *Ruby* at Tusket Wedge, now Wedgeport, while the vessel was loading lumber. This is probably the best photograph of a Yarmouth vessel in the Archives' collection—every plank in the *Ruby's* hull can be seen, as can the joint where the main upper topsail yard has been "fished." The *Ruby*, 1,392 tons and 203 feet in length, was built at Church Point, Nova Scotia, in 1878 for Abel C. Robbins. She sailed in the Yarmouth fleet until about 1900 when she was sold to the Norwegians. She was lost at Fernandina, Florida, in 1907. The life of thirty-one years was quite good for a wooden vessel.
George Parker photograph

BARQUE *H.B. CANN*

BOTTOM RIGHT: This vessel was built on Yarmouth Harbour in 1881 for the Canns of Yarmouth: H. Cann, H. B. Cann, C. W. Cann, Lyman E. Cann, and Rudolph Cann, her first master. She travelled the world visiting ports such as Shanghai, Victoria (BC), New York, and Hamburg, ending her days in 1895 on the rocks of Wolf Island, Labrador. In this photograph, taken in some unknown port the *H. B. Cann* is tied to a snow-covered wharf with a small raft/workshop alongside.

RUBY

H.B. CANN

SHIP
STALWART

The original of this photograph, probably taken in 1890, may have been an advertisement for the dry dock company as evidenced by the wording on the card backing: "Ship *Stalwart*, of Yarmouth, N.S. 1545 Tons. Capt. G. B. Cann, In the Provincial Dry Dock, Pier 2, Erie Basin, Brooklyn. Vessels docked at any time of Tide. Telephone Call, No 502. Bruce & Gorham, Photo., 659 Fulton St., Brooklyn." The cleanliness of the ship's bottom suggests the vessel had just been "metalled," the process of covering the hull below the waterline with "yellow metal" to prevent toredo worms from attacking the hull. The *Stalwart* was built at Barton, Nova Scotia, in 1885 for Jacob Bingay and others. In 1900 she was sold to Spanish interests for £4,300, was renamed *Remedios Pascual*, and was lost off Shipbottom, New Jersey, while on a voyage from Argentina with a cargo of bones.

**BARQUE
BOWMAN
B. LAW**

Ordered by William Law & Co. from builders in Dumbarton, Scotland, in 1885, the *Bowman B. Law* was Yarmouth's first iron vessel (and Canada's second iron square-rigger). The Yarmouth County Museum Archives owns the "specification book" for this vessel which gives an amazing amount of information about her construction and her initial outfit of supplies. The *Bowman B. Law* circled the world five times, carrying a variety of cargoes. The vessel was finally lost to fire at Tegal, Java, in October 1901. This portrait photograph was taken in San Francisco by Mr. Wilton, marine photographer. The painted "gunports" along the ship's side were, by the 1880s, quite fashionable, and were not to fool pirates into thinking she was an armed vessel, as was the original intent of such a paint scheme. The *Bowman B. Law* was named after the owner's son who became a Member of Parliament for Yarmouth and was the only MP who died in the fire that destroyed the Parliament buildings in 1916.

Lillian A. Robbins

Baldwin

**SHIP
LILLIAN L.
ROBBINS**

TOP LEFT: Taken by a McLennon & Co. photographer of Greenock, Scotland, this photograph shows the ship at anchor when she was brand new, having been built recently in the Russell & Co. yards in that Clydebank city in 1892. For the next five years the ship plied between New York and the Orient. Built of steel, she was the pride of Yarmouth's dwindling fleet of square-riggers. Owned by John Y. Robbins, George Sanderson, and others, the *Lillian L. Robbins* was named for Robbins' wife. Her first master was Evelyn E. Robbins, the first cousin of the principal owner. In 1897 her name was changed to *Ancenis*; in the early 1900s she was sold to the Norwegians who changed her name to *Staut* in 1920 and operated her until later in the decade.

BARQUENTINE *BALDWIN*

BOTTOM LEFT: In this photograph the *Baldwin* is shown on the Yarmouth Marine Railway slip. Built at Meteghan, Nova Scotia, in 1891 the *Baldwin* was constructed specifically to carry locomotives to Argentina. Named for the Baldwin Locomotive Company of the United States, she carried two of their locomotives at a time in her hold. Being rigged as a barquentine, with less rigging than a barque or a full-rigged ship, was undoubtedly of considerable advantage when it came to loading and unloading such large and heavy cargoes. Other cargoes later carried by this vessel were mahogany wood for New York, coal for Yarmouth, lumber for Buenos Aires, linseed for Europe, and salt from Turks Island.

**BARQUE
MARY A.
LAW**

Built in 1890 at Meteghan, Nova Scotia, for William Law and others, the vessel was named after Mr. Law's wife. The ship was 890 tons and 185 feet in length. This photograph shows the vessel moored to pilings in the back channel of Yarmouth Harbour. On the extreme right, the skyline shows the Grand Hotel and just under the vessel's bowsprit Beacon House, home of Loran E. Baker. The *Mary A. Law* was among the last of the large wooden square-riggers to be built for Yarmouth shipowners.

STEAMER DOMINION (EX LINDA)

Built in 1864 at Mystic, Connecticut, this vessel may have been a blockade runner during the American Civil War. She was purchased for $65,000 by the Yarmouth and Boston Steamship Company in 1866 as the *Linda*, for the Yarmouth-Boston run. Her name was changed, in 1873 to *Dominion* after she was refloated from a grounding at Chegoggin, near Yarmouth. She continued on the Boston run until she was lost on Big Duck Island in 1893. There was no loss of life.

SS ROBERT G. CANN

Between late 1800 and mid 1900 Hugh Cann & Son's Cann Line carried passengers and freight to ports around Nova Scotia and across the Bay of Fundy to many ports. The steamer *Robert G. Cann* was built in Shelburne, Nova Scotia, in 1911 and served the company until she foundered in a storm in the Bay of Fundy one winter night in 1946, taking with her Captain Emery Peters and his crew. This 1911 photograph shows her newly painted tied up at the Killam Brothers' wharf. *Parker photograph*

Yarmouth to Boston steamers

ss YARMOUTH

This ship was the first vessel built expressly for service between Yarmouth and Boston. Built in Dumbarton, Scotland, in 1887 she was claimed to be "the finest steamer plying between the United States and the Maritime Provinces." She had berths for 350 passengers, had electric lighting, and her speed was guaranteed at 14 knots. Her original cost was $120,000. Three years later the *Yarmouth* was joined by the *Boston*, both vessels being employed by the Yarmouth Steamship Company in carrying passengers and freight between the ports from which the ships derived their respective names. The *Yarmouth* later ran on the Digby to Saint John run for many years and was eventually sold to a New York group whose intention was to colonize Liberia with American blacks. The scheme failed, and the *Yarmouth* was dismantled in Philadelphia in 1922. In this photograph passengers stroll near the wheelhouse while the mate leans on the window sill.

ss PRINCE ARTHUR

In 1894 the various Annapolis Valley route railways from Halifax to Yarmouth amalgamated to form the Dominion Atlantic Railway (D. A. R.). Wanting to own steamers for the Boston run, the directors ordered two new steamers to be built in Hull, England, and went into competition with the Yarmouth Steamship Company. These two vessels, the *Prince George* and the *Prince Arthur* arrived in Yarmouth in 1898 and 1899, respectively. Fitted with twin screws they were capable of 20 knots. Competition intensified between the two companies, driving fares down to an astounding $0.75 for the Yarmouth to Boston trip. Eventually the railway won and acquired the steamship company's vessels but their fleet was later sold to the Eastern Steamship Corporation. During the First World War, both the *Prince Arthur* and the *Prince George* served with the British Admiralty; they later returned to service out of Yarmouth and were broken up in the late 1920s.

Life At Sea—Deck Scenes

CAPTAIN ISAAC WEBSTER

Captain Webster is shown here aboard the four-masted barque *Iranian* taking a sun sight in order to calculate his position. The *Iranian* was carrying a load of kerosene or "case oil" (oil in five-gallon containers packed two to a wooden crate) from Bayonne, New Jersey, to Yokohama, Japan. The Captain's informal attire— a string belt and bare feet—suggests he is perfectly at home. After five months at sea, Captain Webster died shortly before the ship entered Yokohama, where he was buried. The Yarmouth County Museum Archives has a series of photos taken in 1896/1897 by Dr. Charles A. Webster who was aboard for health reasons.

OLD CAMERON AT THE WHEEL

In this dramatic photograph Cameron, one of the crew of the *Iranian*, is seen in his oilskins and leather sea boots steering the vessel. The wheelbox behind the large ship's wheel contains the steering mechanism; below it the emergency steering tiller is visible.

SS BARON BELHAVEN The caption to this professional photograph reads "SS *Baron Belhaven* of Ardrossan, J. F. Corning, Commander, 3550 Tons. H.P.1250. New York, June 19th, 1888." The positions of the several crew members in the photo are given as: (left to right) Steward, Cook, 2nd Mate, 3rd Engineer, 1st Engineer, Chief Mate, and 2nd Engineer. Presumably there was no need to identify Captain Corning at the top of the ladder and his three children. By the 1880s, the decline of the Yarmouth fleet forced Yarmouth captains to look for work elsewhere. In this case, Captain Corning found a job commanding a steamer which was registered in Ardrossan, Scotland. Judging from the spindles on the ladder and the trim of the woodwork, a fine steamer it was, too.

Life At Sea—Interiors

SALOON OF THE SOKOTO

This photograph shows a Yarmouth master in a British vessel. Captain Percy Crosby and wife are shown in the after saloon of the four-masted barque *Sokoto* of Liverpool, England. The photograph was taken in Japan in 1901. Since interior photographs of ships are quite rare, it is a real gem. Ample detail is visible, including family photos, a gramophone, decorative wicker chairs, a family album, the sliding and gimballed oil lamp, rails on the sideboard to keep things in place at sea, and two bird cages. The *Sokoto* was built in Port Glasgow, Scotland, in 1887. Approximately thirty years later, during the First World War, she was sunk by a submarine off Cape Wrath, Scotland.

CABIN OF THE ABYSSINIA

This is one of the most interesting nautical photographs in the Archives' collection, showing the cabin interior of the barque *Abyssinia* of Saint John, New Brunswick, with (master) Captain Arthur Hilton's daughter, Marion, and his sister-in-law Edna Williams. Captain Hilton's wife, Cora, was an amateur photographer, trained by George Parker of Yarmouth. Her sister, Edna, had been sent to sea by her family who thought that she was "seeing too much of the wrong man." A painting of the *Abyssinia* is in the background. This went with the vessel when it was sold to Italian owners in 1904.

The barque *Belmont* was Yarmouth's last square-rigger. Built of steel in Glasgow, Scotland in 1891 she was commanded for many years by Captain Frederick A. Ladd. He took his family to sea with him, and his two children, Forrest and Kathryn, grew up at sea. The *Belmont* had a long life, surviving the First World War during which many sailing ships were destroyed by German submarines. She was eventually converted to a coal barge and was sunk in Florida in 1933.

INTERIOR SHOT OF THE BELMONT

This photograph of the saloon of the *Belmont* shows the luxurious conditions in which Captain Ladd and his family lived for many years. Note the fireplace which would not have been lit at sea in anything but the calmest conditions. Another photo in the archives' collection shows a piano at the opposite end of the cabin. The saloon walls appear to have inlaid bird's eye maple panelling, carpets cover the floor, and all the furniture is upholstered. Light was provided, in the daytime, by a large skylight and, in the evening, by an overhead oil lamp. While cabin interior photographs are rare, those of the crews' quarters are even rarer—it would be interesting to see a comparison.

Tale of two children

This series of three snapshots, taken at sea aboard the *Belmont*, show, in the first one, Captain Ladd's two children, Kathryn and her much older brother, Forrest, along with the family dog, Pilot. (A "pilot" in nautical parlance is someone who is hired to safely take a vessel into and out of a given port.)

WORK TIME

Kathryn did not waste her time at sea; she helped with the chores. In this picture she is shown scrubbing the deck and helping one of the sailors polish the binnacle cover and other pieces of brass. She liked this job and often assisted with the brass polishing at the Yarmouth County Museum in later years.

DRESS-UP TIME

This picture was taken on the deck of the *Belmont*. Kathryn was dressed up in her father's sou'wester and sea boots. Mrs. Ladd's letters to her father have provided us with a marvellous idea of what life at sea was like for a mother and her small children.

Wrecks and Disasters

THE SS CASTILIAN The steamer *Castilian* was wrecked on Gannet Rock Ledges, off Yarmouth, on March 12, 1899, on her maiden voyage while returning from Portland, Maine, to Liverpool, England. Her 52 passengers and 104 crew were all saved, although the ship eventually became a total wreck. In this photograph salvagers remove cargo and any other items of value from the wreckage. Judging from the paintings of the wreck, which was surrounded with vessels of all sizes, the ship was thoroughly "cleaned" before she broke up. Items from the ship ended up in many homes along the coast of Yarmouth County, and over the years many of these items have found their way to the Yarmouth County Museum whose collection contains such artifacts as saloon chairs and table, dinnerware and cutlery, a mirror, life preserver, binnacle light, bucket, bunk cover, and even one of the *Castilian's* nameplates.

PADDLE STEAMER CITY OF MONTICELLO

This vessel foundered five miles west of Yarmouth Cape on November 10, 1900. Thirty-six of the forty people aboard died, making this one of Yarmouth's greatest shipping tragedies. When the *Monticello* arrived at Cape Forchu, off Yarmouth Harbour, the wind was strong out of the northwest, the waves were high, and the vessel was listing from water in her hold. Unable to get her head around to head for the harbour, the water eventually put out the boilers and the engines stopped. Three boats were launched, one capsized immediately, a second made it to shore but only four of its passengers survived, and the third boat was also lost. The tragedy left fifteen widows and forty-nine fatherless children.

SS MIRA

The steamer *Mira* ran aground at Chebogue Point, Yarmouth County, on February 3, 1902. The vessel was heading for Louisbourg, Cape Breton when she went ashore in a blinding snow squall, having mistaken Cape Forchu Light for Cape Sable Light. All hands survived. The huge size of the vessel can be appreciated by comparing her with the men and ox carts at the bottom of the ladder.

BARQUE
KING
MALCOLM

When the *King Malcolm* grounded at High Head, Short Beach, in July 1914 she was likely the last square-rigger to go ashore in southwestern Nova Scotia. Many details are visible in this excellent photograph, including the "Jacob's ladder" hanging down over the port bow as well as two crewmen aloft on the main topgallant yard. The *King Malcolm* had a hole cut in her side, her sand ballast was removed by ox team. The hole was patched and the vessel pulled off and towed to Halifax where she spent the war as a coal barge transferring coal to naval vessels. *George Parker photograph*

SS NORTH STAR

On August 8, 1919, in a thick fog, the steamer *North Star* was carrying passengers from Boston to Yarmouth when she foundered on shoals near the harbour entrance in calm seas. All passengers and crew were landed safely, but the ship could not be salvaged and eventually broke up. Its wreck is still a favourite site for local divers. Several artifacts from this ship, including the wheel and bell are now proudly displayed at the Yarmouth County Museum.

LURCHER LIGHTSHIP

One of the navigational aids to prevent shipwreck was the *Lurcher* lightship—a floating lighthouse which marked the Lurcher Shoals to the west of Yarmouth Harbour. This particular vessel, built in Toronto in 1903, was on station from February 1904 to 1951 as a result of a petition made to the government by the Saint John Board of Trade. Her crew for most of that time did a shift of one month on, one month off aboard the *Lurcher*.

**SS
PRINCE
GEORGE**

This photograph of the Yarmouth to Boston steamer *Prince George* shows some of the storm damage sustained by the ship on one of her July 1919 crossings to Boston. Notice how large seas have played havoc with some of the ship's lifeboats. One of her lifeboats was washed away by a giant wave that towered above the ship's bridge and which, when it hit, pushed the ship almost onto her side, throwing passengers and crew from their bunks and causing a great deal of damage. The woman surveying the damage is one of the stewardesses. The large double wheel is the vessel's emergency steering wheel.

Chapter 8

Transportation

GOOD FOR WHATEVER AILS YOU

This photograph shows the replacement for the horse-drawn vehicle that advertised Minard's Liniment which was first produced in Hants Country in the 1860s by Dr. Minard. In 1887 C. C. Richards (druggist) and Captain Augustus Cann purchased the rights to produce the liniment. In 1905 the business became a joint stock company known as Minard's Liniment Co. Ltd. That year marked a record business with sales of 310,000 bottles, attributable in large measure to advertisements placed in nearly eight hundred newspapers and magazines. In 1967 the business was sold and moved elsewhere.

In this postcard, published by Edgar J. Vickery of Yarmouth from a photograph taken by one of the Parkers, local character Roland Crocker is leading his dagon ox and cart along Main Street. His cargo, a barrel, is lashed down to avoid spilling its contents. Oxen usually worked in teams of two; when one was used alone it was termed a "dagon ox."

**OFF TO
WORK**

Three teams of oxen hitched to their wagons with teamsters alongside are ready for work; a small group of spectators follow behind. One can almost hear the bell hung around the neck of the first ox at right as they step off.

**LIFEBOAT
AND
HORSES**

Little is known about this photograph of two men driving five horses that are pulling a lifeboat. The cart is obviously made especially for the lifeboat named *Reward* and is also marked CLSS (probably Canadian Life Saving Service). The arrangement of the horses, two ahead and three behind, is unusual.

**THIRTY-
FOUR
WAGON
WHEELS**

Is this a party or a wagon sale? Seven wagons of different types are shown in this delightful photograph. There is a horse hitched to one wagon and most of the men appear to be in work clothes carrying some type of wool. (For those who tried to count thirty-four wagon wheels, two are just visible behind the fence to the right of the house.)

GAVEL'S BRIDGE, GAVELTON

This scenic photograph could be ordered from the photographer by quoting its number: 348. Undoubtedly the drivers and passengers of the two horse-drawn vehicles on the bridge would have ordered one or more. This bridge, built in the late 1800s, crosses the Tusket River at Gavelton. *L. G. Swain photograph*

THREE STAGE-COACHES ON CLIFF STREET

These three coaches, loaded with passengers, are about to leave from the corner of Cliff and Kirk Streets. The passengers' clothing suggests they may be on a special excursion. The coach in the foreground is probably the one presently owned by the Nova Scotia Museum and on display at Uniacke House.

BELOW: Milton Corner, with the Cann, Allen & Co. store in the background, makes a delightful backdrop to this photograph of an overcrowded omnibus. Note the pails and other containers hanging on the outside of the store. Alexander Bain started his omnibus service from Milton Corner to Moody's Corner (Main and Argyle Streets) in 1878. It operated until the introduction of the electric street railway in 1892. *L. G. Swain photograph*

BAIN'S OMNIBUS

ROZEE'S MODEL BAKERY

Not to be confused with James Rozee, Sr., confectioner at 274 Main Street, James Rozee, Jr. had his Bakery and Confectionary at 131 and 253 Main Street. Sitting in front of his Model Bakery in his delivery cart, possibly with James Rozee, Jr. standing proudly alongside. Judging from the "Welcome" pennants sporting a Union Jack in the store windows, this photograph may have been taken in 1894 when Governor General Lord Aberdeen visited Yarmouth.

SIGHTSEEING IN THE SUBURBS

The advertising on the reverse side of this c. 1910 photograph reads: "This automobile is for the use of the traveling public and makes two trips every day to Port Maitland by the Sea, leaving Yarmouth at 10 A.M. and at 2:30 P.M. Around the town, seeing Yarmouth's most attractive points, Residential Streets, Parks, Reservoir, Milton Lakes, etc., making a complete circuit of the town, at 8 A.M. and 1:30 P.M. Automobile on the wharf at arrival of steamers. Engage your seats early. Tickets sold at all the Hotels. Baker's automobile service."

Early Community Advertising

The Yarmouth Street Railway, started in 1892, was the first in the Maritimes. In this scene the streetcar is at the northern end of the line, a little beyond Milton Corner. The sign on the front of the car reads: "Disney A. M. E. Church. Annual Picnic. Wednesday August 29th. Sand Beach. Admission 10¢. Come."

BASEBALL TRAILER

When the Yarmouth Gateways went off to win the Nova Scotia Amateur Baseball Championship for the third time in 1934 they traveled to Cape Breton in this trailer. It is shown attached via a "fifth wheel" to the Hudson which was driven for many years by Pete LeBlanc. The car and trailer, originally brought to Yarmouth by H. H. Raymond for his exclusive use, is shown in front of Trefry's Garage, Central Street. The car, trailer, and garage were, at the time, owned by the Taylor Brothers.

Photographers
and their Subjects

DORITT HORTON

This photograph of Doritt Horton in her Yarmouth studio shows a
self-confident young woman surrounded by interesting memorabilia.
It is not known if this is a self-portrait.

Llewellyn Swain

Born in the Barbados in 1827, Llewellyn G. Swain and his family moved to Yarmouth in 1853, where he set up shop as a clock- and watchmaker and jeweller. By 1860 his business had expanded to include musical instruments, perfume, and toys. Four years later he had opened a variety store. In 1866 Swain auctioned off his watches and jewellery and began again as a photographer producing cartes des visites, ambrotypes, and tin types in a suite of rooms over the variety store at the corner of Cliff and Main Streets. For the next few years Swain re-opened and closed his watchmaking business several times and travelled to local villages with his photography business.

In 1883 a hitherto unheard of son, Llewellyn C. Swain, arrived from Boston to take over his father's business, but by the time of the senior Swain's death in 1894, a brother-in-law, A. R. Doe, had been running the photography business for "some time." Doe is recorded as a photographer in the 1895 Directory, but by 1907 Mrs. A. R. Doe indicated that Mr. Doe had died, and that the business of Swain's Photography had ceased.

TRADEMARK CARTES DES VISITES

In this typical example of Swain's work, an unknown woman wears an interesting jacket over her dress and "her" family photo album sits close at hand.

UNKNOWN BOY

This photograph shows that although Swain was something of a "jack of all trades," he was an accomplished photographer. The clarity and lighting here make a very fine photograph.

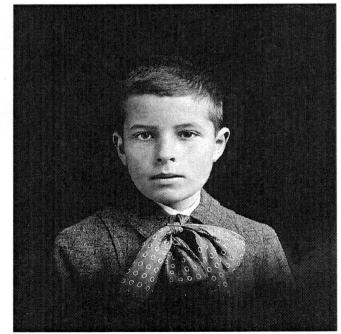

George Parker

George Fletcher Parker was born in 1851. According to the 1890 Yarmouth Directory, he had established himself as "the Yarmouth Photographer" at the age of thirty-nine. His studio was expensively appointed with elegant furnishings and modern equipment. A great deal of emphasis was placed on the card backs of his photographs, which were decorated with intricate etchings.

After making such a fine start in the photography field, George left the business to become one of the best-known publicity men in Eastern North America. After joining the Dominion Atlantic Railway as Passenger Agent, Parker affiliated himself with various tourist and steamship agencies and travelled extensively. He is credited with enthusiastically promoting this region and greatly raising Yarmouth's profile in the United States. Parker Studios was left in the capable hands of a younger brother, Enos, who continued to flourish in the photography business.

George Parker died on June 14, 1932, at the age of eighty-one in Connecticut. He is buried in Yarmouth's Mountain Cemetery.

HILDA ALLEN

ABOVE: Looking almost as though she is ready for a nap, such a staged pose seems unusual from a child so young.

ALICE, EVELYN, AND MILDRED WETMORE

RIGHT: This lovely photograph captures the personalities of the beguiling children of Captain George L. Wetmore and his wife, Marion Allen. None of these three sisters ever married, and all had lifelong interests in the Yarmouth County Historical Society.

THREE UNIDENTIFIED WOMEN

An interesting example of the attention George Parker paid to posing, this well-balanced photo highlights the wonderfully detailed clothing of the 1870s. The dress with the "bishops sleeves" is actually from an earlier period. The bonnets, shawls, and bags warrant a close look.

EDWARD ROSS PARKER

RIGHT: The son of Edward F. and Jessie Bremner Ross was born in Yarmouth on December 4, 1879. Although he worked as a banker he is better remembered for his yacht *Spray*, built to his own design and a successful cup winner in 1897. The Yarmouth County Museum has this cup in its collection, and it is still symbolically presented at the recently resurrected annual "Yarmouth Cup" Ocean Race. Parker moved to Mandeville, British West Indies, to manage a branch of the Bank of Nova Scotia. He contracted typhoid fever there and died in 1909 at the age of thirty. He is buried in the Mandeville Cemetery.

These photographs illustrate George Parker's penchant for elaborate sets. Clearly artistic, Parker placed his subjects in imaginative settings, and balanced each photograph beautifully. The use of rope and ivy attest to Parker's attention to detail. Unfortunately, the subjects in these photographs remain unidentified.

Enos Parker

Enos Rogers Parker, Yarmouth's best-known photographer, was born in 1864, one of nine children and the younger brother by thirteen years to George Parker. Enos began his career by apprenticing under George, who had already established a studio across from the Lorne Hotel on Main Street. Both brothers are noted as working together in the 1890 and 1895 Town Directories. The 1907 Directory records Enos working on his own and George as the "Passenger Agent" for the Dominion Atlantic Railway.

Enos Parker went on to have a very distinguished and prolific career as an independent photographer spanning over twenty years. In Yarmouth the Parker name is synonymous with quality photography; Parker photos are artistic and well made. In the studio Parker placed great emphasis on proper setting and interesting props; his scenic views were always well balanced and beautifully proportioned. Enos Parker died on February 17, 1918, at the age of fifty-four while still in the prime of his career.

MARIA BROWN

The beautiful daughter of Captain John A. Tilley is shown here wearing stunning "walking out" attire with fox stole and intricately detailed hat. No props or backdrops were necessary for this lovely shot taken at the turn of the century. (See the photograph of Maria and her husband, Charles F. Brown, on page 111.)

The handwritten inscription on the back of this photograph says: "L. Wolseley Bingay and Irving R. Tooker turned in for the night in the veldt in the Transvaal during the war between Great Britain and the South African Republic. 1900." In fact, Bingay and Tooker are safely curled up in Parker's Yarmouth Studio. (See the image in Special Events of Bingay's triumphant return home from the Boer War.) Tooker, too, made it home safely and was given a similar reception by the town a few weeks later. After reaching the rank of Captain, Bingay was killed in the First World War while going to the aid of a wounded comrade; he was only thirty-eight. In another sad twist of fate, Osborne Perry, the twenty-six-year-old soldier Bingay saved, was killed in action only five months later.

SLEEPING BENEATH THE STARS

Parker Studios

For a period of time some Yarmouth photos were marked simply "Parker," undistinguished by either George or Enos. It is uncertain exactly what period they represent: either the beginning stages of George's career, or perhaps the transition between George and Enos.

MAN AND HIS DOG

This unidentified man sports a lengthy beard and is wearing his buttoned knickers and stockings ready for a ride on his penny farthing, accompanied by his faithful pug.

MR. AND MRS. CHARLES FREDERICK BROWN

Charles was the son of Charles Edward and the grandson of the Honourable Stayley Brown. He was the manager of the Yarmouth Amalgamated Telephone Company. Married on December 21, 1896, the couple lived on Clements Avenue with their Saint Bernard shown here.

Yarmouth Portrait Company

Unfortunately, not much is known about the Yarmouth Portrait Company. The first reference we were able to find was a business card which notes that they were "Photographers and Artists" located at 267 Main Street. This card was placed in the Yarmouth Post Office cornerstone on September 1, 1885, and indicated that the business was certainly up and running at that time. They are not noted in the 1890 Directory but appear from 1895–1908. George B. Hall was the proprietor and presumably the photographer and artist at that time.

The company does not appear in further directories but there is no doubt that they were active until at least the mid-1930s.

During these latter years the company was owned by Robert Guest, a druggist. The studios changed location and were above Guest's Hardware Store on Main Street for a time, and also across the street. The photographer is remembered as William Perry, believed to be a single man who boarded with the Churchill family on Carleton Avenue. He is also remembered for his fine hand tinting. Little else is known about Perry. He personally did not sign the photos; they were all noted as being the Yarmouth Portrait Company. Although people still remember William Perry, he left no paper trail behind.

POSED YOUNG MAN

Wearing an elaborate eyelet collar with matching cuffs, this young man sits primly in front of a softly patterned backdrop.

MATCHING DUO

This young mother and her child are perfectly matched both in their clothing and in proportion. The photographer wisely chose to use a solid black backdrop so the subjects stand out.

READY FOR A STROLL

This lovely child in her high bonnet and lace-fringed cape is ready for brisk weather.

Gordon Hatfield

Gordon Sullivan Hatfield was born in the rural community of Tusket Falls, Yarmouth County, in 1871. He was a professional photographer early in his career and managed to combine photography with farming. He owned a considerable amount of land in the area and later became successful as a commercial grower of strawberries and blueberries. He owned real estate on Main Street in Yarmouth and maintained other business interests in the town.

His photography career lasted about fifteen years, from approximately 1900–1915. He was operating a full studio across from his house in the village of Tusket by 1903. An added attraction in the studio was an ice cream parlour operated by Mrs. Chase Hatfield.

Hatfield didn't always sign his work, but many of his studio shots can be identified by his distinctive backdrop. No self-portraits have yet

EGBERT CHESLEY ALLEN AND FRIEND

c. 1900

turned up. Nor is there a known portrait of his wife, Nettie as a married woman, nor one of their home.

It is unclear why Hatfield abandoned photography either as a hobby or as a business around 1915 at the time of his marriage. When he began photography about 1900, the type of camera he used was already obsolete and smaller cameras with spools of film inside had been developed as early as 1890. In 1944 Gordon Hatfield died suddenly at the age of seventy-three from a heart attack brought on while cranking his Model-T truck.

Chesley (on left) was born in 1882 making him approximately eighteen at the time of this photograph taken in Hatfield's Tusket studio. Chesley became a professor at the School for the Blind in Halifax, and was a naturalist and poet. He was the father of Charlie and Fernald, (shown on page 64), and died an untimely death in 1946 at the age of sixty-four.

FAMILY PORTRAIT

It is the distinctive backdrop used in this simple portrait of an unidentified family that identifies this as Hatfield's work. The three-dimensional image is deceiving as the backdrop is in fact linear.

Doritt Horton

Doritt Corning Horton was born in Yarmouth in 1884 and was formally trained in Boston by the well-known portrait artist Chalmers C. Murray. Doritt married Stanley Horton, and their home on the corner of Collins and Second Streets contained her studio and darkroom. It was a happy, interesting household, bustling with gatherings of artists, writers, and musicians from around the world. Portraits were taken in the living room and developed in the basement. Instead of using a timer for developing, Horton simply counted out loud.

BOY WITH "LITTLE RIVER" PUP 1946

This portrait of an unidentified child with his puppy clearly illustrates Horton's trademark soft style. The puppy is a "Little River Duck Dog," now the official provincial dog and recognized as the Nova Scotia Duck Tolling Retriever. These dogs, one of only four uniquely Canadian breeds, were developed and bred in the Little River Harbour area of Yarmouth County.

Her work had a unique ethereal quality that is easy to recognize. She won many awards for her photography and was a talented artist, working in oils, watercolours, and pen and ink.

Doritt Horton was a popular person and was a much sought-after photographer. Some equate her popularity with the demise of the Yarmouth Portrait Company as she came to be regarded as the local photographer of choice. Yarmouth's first major female photographer passed away on April 28, 1951, at the age of sixty-seven.

ALLIE (ALBERT) LABRADOR

A well-known fishing and hunting guide, Allie Labrador lived at the Starr's Road Mi'kmaq Reserve. In this 1936 portrait he is wearing his guiding costume, an interesting mix of Mi'kmaq and Plains Indian styles. When Allie moved to Maine to pick blueberries he gave his costume to Gordon L. Cann, the local government Indian Agent. Cann passed it down to his son Earle, who donated it to the Yarmouth County Museum. In 1995 Allie's grandson Robert Lane and his family visited from Maine and were delighted to see photos and Allie's costume displayed prominently in the museum. The family had spent many years trying to locate Allie's treasured costume and came across it unexpectedly on this chance encounter.

A Bicycle built for Two

These two well-dressed young men, jauntily pose on a two-seated Massey-Harris bicycle set up in Parker's studio, c. 1890. Frank Robbins is on the rear seat, while his friend, Bill Power of Toronto, takes the lead.